NATIONAL GEOGRAPHIC | **GLOBAL ISSUES**

# ENERGY
# RESOURCES

**Andrew J. Milson, Ph.D.**
Content Consultant
University of Texas at Arlington

## Acknowledgments

Grateful acknowledgment is given to the authors, artists, photographers, museums, publishers, and agents for permission to reprint copyrighted material. Every effort has been made to secure the appropriate permission. If any omissions have been made or if corrections are required, please contact the Publisher.

Instructional Consultant: Christopher Johnson, Evanston, Illinois

Teacher Reviewer: Andrea Wallenbeck, Exploris Middle School, Raleigh, North Carolina

## Photographic Credits

**Front Cover, Inside Front Cover, Title Page** ©Chris McKay/National Geographic Stock. **3** (bg) ©Manoj Shah/Stone/Getty Images. **4** (bg) ©Deepol/Rudi Sebastian/plainpicture. **6** (bg) ©Roger Eritja/Alamy. **8** (bg) Mapping Specialists. **10** (bg) ©Axiom Photographic Limited/Superstock. **11** (bl) ©Panoramic Images/Getty Images. **12** (bg) ©Irudi Etcheverry/Alamy. (tc) ©DPA/Zuma Press. **14** (tr) ©Diego Giudice/Corbis. **15** (bg) ©Diego Giudice/Archivolatino/Redux. **16** (bg) ©Pete Turner/Riser/Getty Images. **17** (cl) Mapping Specialists. **19** (bg) ©Rob Howard/Corbis. **20** (t) ©AFP/Getty Images/Newscom. **21** (cr) ©Li Zhen/Xinhua/Landov. **22** (bg) ©Andrew Castellano. **23** (bl) ©Thomas Culhane/Solar Cities. **24** (cr) ©Andrew Castellano. **25** (bg) ©Andrew Castellano. **27** (t) ©Bob Daemmrich/Corbis. **28** (tr) ©David R. Frazier Photolibrary, Inc./Alamy. **30** (tr) ©Roger Eritja/Alamy. (br) ©Irudi Etcheverry/Alamy. **31** (bg) ©Manoj Shah/Stone/Getty Images. (br) ©Lester Lefkowitz/Getty Images. (bl) ©Jane Sweeney/Robert Harding World Imagery/Corbis. (tr) ©Diego Giudice/Corbis.

MetaMetrics® and the MetaMetrics logo and tagline are trademarks of MetaMetrics, Inc., and are registered in the United States and abroad. The trademarks and names of other companies and products mentioned herein are the property of their respective owners. Copyright © 2010 MetaMetrics, Inc. All rights reserved.

Visit National Geographic Learning online at www.NGSP.com.

Visit our corporate website at www.cengage.com.

Printed in the USA.

RR Donnelley, Menasha, WI

ISBN: 978-07362-97608

14 15 16 17 18 19 20 21 22

10 9 8 7 6 5 4 3

# ENERGY TO POWER THE WO

Energy production in Hamburg, Germany, has filled the skies with air pollution.

**ld**

## WHY ARE COUNTRIES AROUND THE WORLD LOOKING FOR NEW ENERGY RESOURCES?

Did you know that decayed plants and tiny creatures from millions of years ago provide most of the energy we use today? They form types of **fossil fuels** that include oil, coal, and natural gas. Fossil fuels provide energy to run everything from computers to jet planes to electric power plants. The problem is that fossil fuels are **nonrenewable energy**. We can't make more of them, and eventually they will be used up. Fossil fuels also cause pollution and add to global climate change. As a result, scientists are looking for alternative energy sources.

# FOSSIL FUEL FACTS

For the past 200 years, we have used fossil fuels as if they would last forever. Every single day, the world burns about 3.6 billion gallons of oil. That's enough to fill almost 122 million bathtubs! New sources of fossil fuels are getting harder to find and extract from the earth.

Producing and burning fossil fuels hurts the environment. Gases released by burning fossil fuels can lead to health problems and air pollution. Gases may contribute to global climate change.

**The Hoover Dam on the Colorado River, one of the largest dams in the world, provides hydroelectric power.**

## WORLD ENERGY USE BY SECTOR

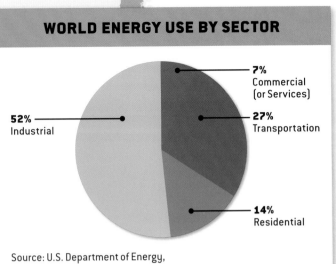

7%
Commercial
(or Services)

52%
Industrial

27%
Transportation

14%
Residential

Source: U.S. Department of Energy,
Energy Information Administration, 2011

## IS THERE AN ALTERNATIVE?

Scientists are looking at sources of **renewable energy** to replace fossil fuels. These are resources that can be used without being used up. Water, sun, wind, and plants are renewable energy sources.

Renewable energy has many advantages. For example, it is almost unlimited. It's cleaner and generally causes little or no pollution. Also, renewable energy sources don't release carbon dioxide ($CO_2$) into the atmosphere. Carbon dioxide is one of the chief causes of air pollution.

## RENEWABLE ENERGY

If renewable energy has all these benefits, then why don't people use more of it? It's difficult and expensive to capture energy from the sun or wind and get it to where it is needed. Most alternative energy is used to make electricity, but most vehicles and power plants use fuel made from oil. In many countries where the need for power is growing, the demand is coming from areas far from established electrical service. That makes finding alternative sources of energy more challenging and urgent.

On the following pages, you will read about how Argentina and Saudi Arabia want to use more renewable energy instead of fossil fuels to power their growth. Using renewable energy sources will aid these countries in expanding their economies and improving the lives of their citizens.

### Explore the Issue

1. **Make Inferences** What are three problems with using fossil fuels?

2. **Draw Conclusions** Why has renewable energy been more expensive than fossil fuels?

# Energy Challeng

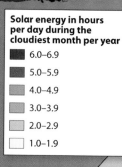

**Solar energy in hours per day during the cloudiest month per year**

- 6.0–6.9
- 5.0–5.9
- 4.0–4.9
- 3.0–3.9
- 2.0–2.9
- 1.0–1.9

NORTH

AMERICA

NORTH ATLANTIC OCEAN

**UNITED STATES** The country has 4.5 percent of the world's population but uses 22 percent of the world's oil. That's more than any other country.

NORTH PACIFIC OCEAN

**MALI** Only 24 percent of the people in Mali have electricity. Without energy resources, it's hard for poor people to improve their lives.

**CASE STUDY 1**

**ARGENTINA** Since 2001, the country's economy has grown faster than its energy resources. Electric companies have a hard time meeting the country's demand.

SOUTH

AMERICA

SOUTH PACIFIC OCEAN

SOUTH ATLANTIC OCEAN

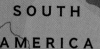

## Explore the Issue

1. **Interpret Maps** Which two continents have the greatest potential for widespread use of solar energy?

2. **Make Predictions** How do you think the decline of oil reserves in Saudi Arabia might affect the United States?

ARCTIC OCEAN

EUROPE

ASIA

NORTH PACIFIC OCEAN

**POLAND** Coal provides 94 percent of Poland's electricity. To reduce pollution, the country could switch to natural gas, but then Poland would have to import it.

### CASE STUDY 2

**SAUDI ARABIA** About one-fifth of all the world's supply of oil is located here. As oil reserves decline, the country must diversify its economy.

AFRICA

INDIAN OCEAN

AUSTRALIA

**NEW ZEALAND** In 2011, one of the worst oil spills in the country's history damaged beaches with hundreds of tons of oil.

N
W E
S

| 0 | 1,000 | 2,000 Miles |
| 0 | 1,000 | 2,000 Kilometers |

ANTARCTICA

9

# ARGENTINA'S
## Sunny Futu

This sculpture in Buenos Aires
follows the sun as it crosses the sky
and is powered by solar energy.

## A BLOSSOMING ECONOMY

A giant metal flower sculpture stands in the United Nations Plaza in Buenos Aires, Argentina. The petals on this moving sculpture open in the sunlight and close at night. This action copies the way many real flowers take in energy from the sun. Argentineans believe that using **solar energy** might help their economy grow even faster in the future. Solar energy comes from the sun's rays that reach Earth.

Argentina is the second largest country in South America, behind Brazil. Argentina's farmers grow more grain than do any other farmers in Latin America. In addition, they export wheat and corn to countries around the world. Factories are busy producing steel, cars, and consumer goods. Tourism and other service businesses employ almost three-fourths of all the workers in Argentina.

## FUELING GROWTH

Farms and factories, hotels and offices all need energy. For now, Argentina has an abundant supply of energy resources, especially natural gas and oil. For the future, though, fuel supplies are far more uncertain. Fossil fuels produce about 90 percent of the country's energy. Although oil and gas production has declined since 1998, Argentina still produces more oil than it needs and exports some to other countries.

Recent discoveries of oil in **shale**, tightly packed sedimentary rock made from mud or clay, might be a new source of oil. However, getting oil out of the shale is more expensive than regular oil drilling. Some people are also concerned about how this drilling might harm the environment.

Argentina also relies on hydroelectric power to produce 25 to 30 percent of its electricity. **Hydroelectric power** uses the energy of moving water. Even with all these resources, Argentina will have a hard time meeting people's future need for energy.

**The lights of cars and buildings and the movement of cars show the expanded use of energy in Argentina's capital, Buenos Aires.**

# Solar panels produce electricity for lighting, heating, cooking, and running appliances—or entire power plants.

Students at the University of Buenos Aires are testing solar cells for use at the school.

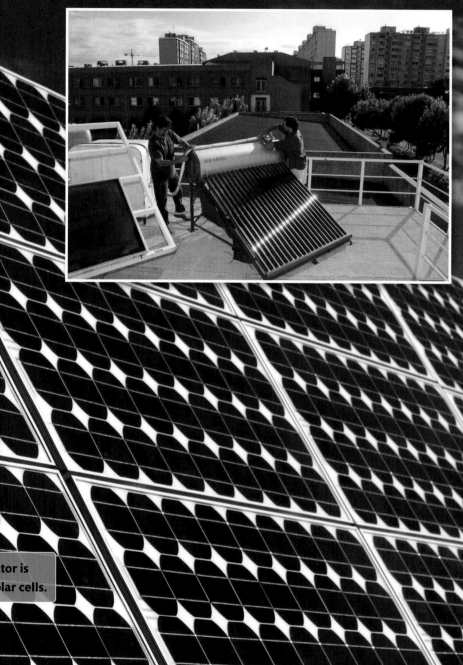

A photovoltaic solar collector is made up of hundreds of solar cells.

## A NEW ENERGY FUTURE

Argentina's leaders know that fossil fuels cause pollution and are nonrenewable. They also know that increasing the use of renewable energy sources is good for Argentina. In 2007, a new law required that 8 percent of the country's energy must come from renewable sources by 2016. These renewable sources are in addition to hydroelectric power.

The country still has a long way to go to reach its goals. In 2010, renewable energy sources such as wind and the sun still produced less than 1 percent of Argentina's energy. The potential, however, is huge. For example, Patagonia in southern Argentina is a very windy region, and the northwestern part of the country has about 300 days of sunshine every year. But how do you turn sunlight or wind into electricity, and how do you store the energy for later use?

## HARNESSING THE SUN'S POWER

The sun is the world's greatest source of energy. Today, it takes about 200,000 truckloads of coal for a power plant to produce the same amount of energy that reaches Earth from the sun each second! However, the amount of the sun's energy that hits any single place at one time is very small. As a result harnessing the sun's power is difficult.

Solar power can be tapped in several ways. The most direct way is to use the sun's heat in a simple solar oven. A reflective surface focuses the power of the sun into a chamber that heats, bakes, or boils food placed in it. You can see an example of that simple equipment on the next page. The advantage to this use of solar power is that it is inexpensive and very mobile, perfect in remote areas. However, this simple equipment doesn't solve the need for larger amounts of power. That requires more complicated equipment.

Another way to collect solar energy is with **photovoltaic cells**, or *solar cells*—devices that change light into electricity. The electricity flows through wires to be used directly or stored in a battery. The power in a single solar cell is just enough to run a battery in a watch or a calculator. Many cells can be combined into solar panels to produce more power. Solar panels produce electricity for lighting, heating, cooking, and running appliances—or entire power plants.

# SOLAR POWER OFF THE GRID

Villages in remote areas of western Argentina are far from the **power grid**. This is the system of cables that distributes electricity from large power plants.

Many villages now generate their own solar power to make people's lives easier. For example, in Jujuy (JOO-jy) province, villagers used to cut 66 pounds of brush each week for cooking and heating. Now, villagers share solar stoves, and some homes have solar water heaters for hot showers.

**A woman in Jujuy province prepares stew using a solar cooker.**

Villagers in Neuquen (nook-win) province relied on generators using gas or oil to heat their schools. Harsh winter conditions meant that all fuel was saved for heating. None was left over for electricity. Photovoltaic (PV) solar panels now keep students warm and run computers.

## EXPANDING SOLAR POWER

Argentina's San Juan province began operating the largest PV power plant in all of South America in 2011. Eventually the site will produce enough power to run 400 to 900 homes for one year and will connect to the country's power grid. It's still a small amount of the province's energy needs, but leaders see it as a big first step.

The San Juan solar plant includes a solar tracking system. "It's like a sunflower, following the position of the sun," says a local man. Soon, more of Argentina's economy may blossom like a flower, tracking the sun and drawing on its power.

## Explore the Issue

1. **Analyze Problems** Why does Argentina need to use renewable energy sources?

2. **Analyze Solutions** Why is solar energy a good way to bring electricity to small villages in Argentina?

Solar panels such as these provide power for villages high in the Andes Mountains of Argentina.

# Saudi Arabia's
# OIL
# WEALT

At an oil refinery in Saudi Arabia, a separation plant burns off excess gas that cannot be refined.

## A SURPRISING DISCOVERY

In 2000 a scientist working for Saudi Aramco, the Saudi Arabian oil company, learned something that surprised him. Sadad Al Husseini (SADD-dadd AL hoo-SAY-nee) had worked for five years studying the world's major oil fields to see how much they produced each year. Then Husseini added in how much new oil fields were expected to produce.

Surprisingly, Husseini concluded that oil production would start leveling off as early as 2004. Then after about 15 years, the amount of oil from traditional sources would start to drop off. This was much sooner than most oil industry experts had predicted. They thought there would be enough oil to meet people's needs for several decades. If Husseini's calculations were correct, the world was going to find it much harder to get the oil it needs to produce gasoline and thousands of other products, including crayons, DVDs, and clothing.

**Saudi Arabia has many gas and oil fields located on the Persian Gulf.**

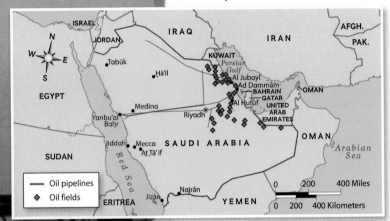

## OIL RULES

Husseini's discovery was especially surprising because it came from Saudi Arabia. Saudi Arabia is the world's second largest producer of oil, behind Russia. It exports more oil than any other country. About one-fifth of the world's known reserves of oil are in Saudi Arabia's vast oil fields. **Oil reserves** are the amount of oil that scientists estimate can be recovered from known sources.

All that oil has made Saudi Arabia wealthy and has transformed the country. When Saudi Arabia was founded in 1932, many of the people were wandering herders who rode on camels. Now most Saudis live in cities and drive cars and SUVs.

About 80 percent of all the money the government takes in comes from oil. This oil **revenue**, or income, has been used to invest in modern transportation and communication systems. It has also helped improve education, health care, and food production.

# WHAT IS "PEAK OIL"?

Saudi scientist Sadad Al Husseini joined other scientists who predicted a peak in the world's oil production. Everyone agrees oil is a nonrenewable resource and that it can't last forever. What people disagree about is when peak oil will occur. The term **peak oil** refers to the time when oil production will reach a maximum and then begin to decline.

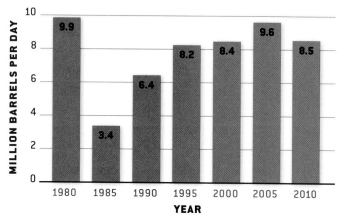

### SAUDI ARABIA CRUDE OIL PRODUCTION

Source: U.S. Energy Information Administration

In 2010, the International Energy Agency (IEA) reported traditional oil production may have peaked in 2006. "The age of cheap oil is over," said the IEA's chief economist.

What facts led to this conclusion? For one thing, total oil production has stayed around 85 million barrels per day for several years. This has not changed even though prices have been higher than ever. In the past, high prices encouraged oil producers to increase their output.

## DEMAND UP—SOLUTIONS NEEDED

When the supply of oil stays level for a time and then declines, the price increases because more people want the limited supply. The U.S. Department of Energy predicted in 2011 that the world demand for energy would increase by 53 percent by 2035. At the same time, the price of oil is expected to rise by about 25 percent. Higher oil prices cause higher transportation costs. That means people pay more for gasoline and for food and other goods.

There are three ways to deal with increased demand for energy. One way is to find new sources and types of fossil fuels. However, it is becoming more difficult and expensive to find and produce them. These fuels also cause more pollution. The second way is to **conserve**, or use less energy. Energy conservation can happen with more efficient motors and appliances. Building design can also create structures that use less fossil fuel energy. The third way is using more renewable energy sources.

The brightly lit capital of Riyadh, Saudi Arabia, shows huge energy use.

The main campus of King Abdullah University houses a super computer which will aid scientific teams in their research.

## MOVING BEYOND OIL

Saudi Arabia has built its whole way of life on oil. But the country's leaders realize that it can't survive unless it becomes less dependent on oil revenue. The government has recognized the need to **diversify**, or broaden, its economy. Examples include investment in factories that produce steel, cement, and fertilizer. Saudis are also exploring other mineral resources in the western parts of the country. The country joined the World Trade Organization to encourage more private companies to do business in Saudi Arabia.

More use of renewable energy is also important to Saudi Arabia's future. The Saudis need to find new ways to meet the growing demand for electricity. Many of the country's communities are far from the main electrical grids and will need to have alternate sources of energy. The Saudis are investigating the use of wind power to generate electricity. Other plans include getting 10 percent of their electricity from solar energy by 2020. Some experts predict that Saudi Arabia could become a center of the solar industry, creating thousands of new jobs.

# INVESTING IN THE FUTURE

In 2009, King Abdullah University of Science and Technology (KAUST) opened in Thuwal, a city on the Red Sea. The university won an international award for its sustainable design. **Sustainable** means using natural resources in a way that preserves them for the future. Solar and wind power keep people cool and water hot. Students travel around the campus using electric vehicles and bicycles. The campus has a high-performance solar electrical system. It has reduced energy usage by 25 percent and water usage by 40 percent or more. These are great achievements in reducing energy usage.

All of these practices are examples of sustainable design. These are just the kinds of steps that will help Saudi Arabia rely less on oil for its energy needs.

Guests at the opening of King Abdullah University of Science and Technology view a model of the university campus. The large photograph shows the actual campus.

## Explore the Issue

1. **Analyze Effects**  How will peak oil affect people around the world?

2. **Draw Conclusions**  Why does Saudi Arabia need to become less dependent on oil?

# Clean Energy
## Improves Lives

T. H. Culhane talks to a resident of
Nairobi, Kenya, about the advantages
of burning biogas instead of corn cobs.

## CITY LIVING OFF THE GRID

In some poor neighborhoods of Cairo, Egypt's capital, a mother spends all day getting water to bathe her family. First, she walks to the water pipe in the center of her neighborhood. After filling her bucket, she walks back with it balanced on her head and climbs three flights of stairs to her apartment. There she dumps the bucket into a pot heating on her stove. She repeats this process many times, until there's enough warm water. When women spend their days this way, they have no time to go to school or work to improve their lives.

Most people in cities in developed countries live "on the grid." This means their homes are connected to electricity and clean running water. When we think of living "off the grid," we usually think of people in rural areas. Could ideas from these rural people help people living without electricity in cities?

## FROM TREETOPS TO ROOFTOPS

That was just the question that National Geographic Emerging Explorer Thomas "T.H." Culhane asked. He saw how people in rain forest villages survived by using every bit of their environment. "It inspired me to rethink urban living along those same ecological principles," Culhane says. In Cairo, he connected with a group called the Zabaleen people who lived in a similar way. They collected the city's garbage by hand. They looked for ways to reuse, recycle, and resell as much waste as possible.

Culhane and a volunteer move a solar water heater into a Cairo neighborhood.

After collecting plastics, the Zabaleen washed the materials and used the sun to dry them for recycling. Culhane began to think about how to use the sun for other things. He knew there was a need to find efficient ways to heat water. He developed plans for a simple solar water heater built from recycled materials. (You can see part of his invention in the smaller picture at the left.) It uses plastic water bottles to hold water to be heated. Since 2003, more than 30 solar water heaters have been installed on rooftops in two different Cairo neighborhoods, the Zabaleen neighborhood and the neighborhood of Darb Al-Ahmar. The two groups work together to share expertise and solve common problems.

# CONNECTING PEOPLE AND IDEAS

Connecting people and ideas to solve problems is the goal of Culhane's nonprofit organization, Solar CITIES. The organization provides money and basic plans, and local people add their skills and creative ideas. By using recycled materials and their own labor, people create solar water heaters they can afford.

Solar CITIES also helps people in Kenya recycle food wastes into gas for cooking and heating. Again Culhane got the idea from working with rural people, this time in India. The biogas reactors he developed use **microbes**, tiny organisms such as germs, taken from animal stomachs to turn the food waste into gas. "In 24 hours, you've got 2 hours of cooking gas from yesterday's cooking garbage," Culhane explains. The gas from the bioreactors is used to generate cooking fuel or run generators to produce electricity. He says "We're cleaning up Kenya using everything AND the kitchen sink."

Students get a close-up view of a biogas reactor at their school.

Culhane's energy solutions are now spreading. Solar water heaters and biogas reactors have been installed in Kenya, Tanzania, Palestine, Israel, Botswana, the United States, Germany, and Nepal. The Solar CITIES team uses Internet videos, a blog, and social networking sites to explain the system. In this way, people around the world can add their own ideas and build on the Solar CITIES project's experience. As Culhane says, "It's just a matter of connecting and letting our collective intelligence work."

## Explore the Issue

1. **Identify Problems and Solutions** Why did T. H. Culhane establish the Solar CITIES project?

2. **Make Inferences** How do Culhane's ideas and inventions benefit the people of Cairo and Kenya?

At fellow Emerging Explorer Kakenya Ntaiya's Dream School in Kenya, Culhane demonstrates an in-sink food grinder. The grinder can turn food scraps into fuel and fertilizer.

"We're cleaning up Kenya using everything AND the kitchen sink."
—T. H. Culhane

# Go on an Energy DIET

## —and report your findings

You don't have to be an inventor to use energy wisely. You just have to care—and get involved. You can identify many ways to save energy at home and at school. By going on an energy diet and taking steps to use less energy, you can make a big difference.

## IDENTIFY

- Make a list of all the ways you use energy at home and at school.

- Talk with your family and classmates to brainstorm ideas for ways to save energy.

- Do some research on the Internet to learn about steps you can take to use less energy.

- Check with your local government or power company to see if they have ideas for saving energy.

## ORGANIZE

- Form a team with 3 to 5 classmates and review National Geographic's Great Energy Challenge.

- Decide what energy-saving measures you will add to your diet each week.

- Check in each week and decide which actions you actually completed.

High school students work on a project to create a solar car.

## DOCUMENT

- Create a list of energy uses at the beginning of the diet and changes you will make to use less energy.

- Check the boxes of the actions you have completed on the Great Energy Challenge worksheet.

- Make video or audio recordings of members of your team discussing their experiences on the energy diet.

## SHARE

- Use your photos and recordings to create a multimedia presentation about your energy diet and share it with your class.

- Write and perform a skit to present to your class or a school assembly about ways to save energy.

- Create public service announcements for your school or a local radio station to encourage others to take specific steps to save energy.

# Write an Argument

Every community is looking for ways to use energy wisely. Projects might involve the energy sources used by the city or options in public transportation. Find out about an energy project in your community. Decide if you are for or against the project. Write an argument either *for* or *against* it.

## RESEARCH

**Use reliable sources such as local media or government sources to research and answer these questions:**

- How will the project affect the community's energy use?
- What are the claims, or arguments, in favor of the project?
- What are the counter-claims, or arguments, against the project?

**As you do your research, be sure to take notes.**

# DRAFT

**Review your notes and then write a first draft.**

- The first paragraph, or introduction, should grab the reader's attention and state your claim, which is your position on the value of the use of certain energy sources or of public transportation.
- Briefly explain what the opposing argument is. Then state that you will show why your argument is stronger.
- The second paragraph, or body, should develop your side of the argument. You should present logical reasons and relevant evidence for your claim about certain energy sources or public transportation in your area.
- In the third paragraph, write a conclusion, which should follow from and support the argument you have presented.

# REVISE & EDIT

**Read your first draft to make sure that it gives persuasive reasons to support your claim.**

- Does your introduction clearly state your argument?
- Does the body support your argument with logical reasons and relevant evidence?
- Does your conclusion support your argument about the use of certain energy sources or public transportation?

**Revise the argument to make sure you have covered all the points. Then check your paper for errors in spelling and punctuation.**

# PUBLISH & PRESENT

**Now you are ready to publish and present your argument. Print out your paper or write a clean copy by hand. Publish your argument as an opinion piece or a letter to the editor in your school or local newspaper.**

# Visual GLOSSARY

**conserve**  *v.*, to use without wasting

**diversify**  *v.*, to broaden or add variety

**fossil fuel**  *n.*, an energy source formed by preserved remains of plants and tiny creatures

**hydroelectric power**  *n.*, electricity created by the energy in moving water

**microbe**  *n.*, a tiny organism, such as a germ

**nonrenewable energy**  *n.*, an energy source that will be used up

**oil reserves**  *n.*, the amount of oil that scientists estimate can be recovered from known sources

**peak oil**  *n.*, the idea that oil production will reach a high point and then begin to decline

**photovoltaic cell**  *n.*, a device that changes light into electricity; also called *solar cell*

**power grid**  *n.*, a system of power plant cables that distributes electricity

**renewable energy**  *n.*, an energy source that can never be used up

**revenue**  *n.*, income used to pay expenses

**shale**  *n.*, sedimentary rock made from mud or clay

**solar energy**  *n.*, energy from the sun

**sustainable**  *adj.*, using natural resources to preserve them for the future

hydroelectric power

photovoltaic cell (solar cell)

sustainable

renewable energy

fossil fuel

# INDEX

# SKILLS